ESSAY PRESS

Letters from Abu Ghraib

JOSHUA CASTEEL *Letters from*
Abu Ghraib ESSAY PRESS

Joshua was a CCU student
1999 - 2000.

ESSAY PRESS IS GRATEFUL TO THE COLLEGE OF
ARTS AND SCIENCES AT OHIO UNIVERSITY
AND TO A NUMBER OF INDIVIDUAL DONORS
FOR THEIR GENEROUS SUPPORT OF THIS PRESS

WWW.ESSAYPRESS.ORG

THE EMAILS COLLECTED IN THIS BOOK ARE
ACTUAL MESSAGES WRITTEN AND SENT BY THE
AUTHOR BETWEEN MAY 2004 AND MARCH 2005.
THEY HAVE BEEN EDITED IN PLACES FOR
CLARITY AND CONCISION, BUT THE INTENT
OF THE AUTHOR AND HIS ORIGINAL MEANING
HAVE REMAINED INTACT IN ALL CASES.

DESIGNED BY QUEMADURA
PRINTED ON ACID-FREE, RECYCLED PAPER
IN THE UNITED STATES OF AMERICA

ISBN 978-0-9791189-3-7
LCCN 2008928478

FIRST EDITION

Foreword

Prison occupies a singular place in the literary imagination as a site of delusion and self-examination, of fear and trembling, of death and redemption. It is difficult to conceive of Western literature without the works of writers in shackles. To rehearse the names of, say, Sir Walter Raleigh, Marquis de Sade, Henry David Thoreau, and Dietrich Bonhoeffer is to be reminded that visions articulated from behind bars may have lasting power. From St. Paul's epistles to Martin Luther King's "Letter from Birmingham Jail," seminal writings, often in the form of correspondence, have issued from the imprisoned; whether they are discussing faith and ethics, poetry and politics, or eros and agape, their true theme is freedom, which has different meanings at different times and places. In post-9/11 America, where the war on terror is a defining feature of the body politic, Joshua Casteel's *Letters from Abu Ghraib* offers readers an opportunity to reflect on the meaning of the most important word in our founding documents. What is liberty anyway?

In the rich tradition of prison literature the writer is usually the prisoner, not the interrogator. But in *Letters from Abu Ghraib* it is the interrogator who speaks from a prison that has come to symbolize the moral depths to which the United States has sunk in its prosecution of the war on terror. Casteel arrived in Iraq six weeks after the revelation, in 2004, of the scandal at Abu Ghraib, where thousands of dissidents had been tortured and executed under Saddam Hussein; after the Iraqi dictator was deposed in the U.S.-led invasion, coalition forces filled the prison with suspected insurgents. But when details emerged, on the television news magazine *Sixty Minutes* and in a *New Yorker* article by Seymour Hersch, of American military police torturing and abusing prisoners, with lurid photographs documenting their cruelty, there was widespread revulsion—which hardly diminished when Arabic linguists like Casteel were sent to Abu Ghraib with orders to extract information legally, in accordance with the Army Field Manual. What Casteel confronted, in his interrogations of Iraqis and of his own soul, was the power of evil; what he discovered, in prayer and readings of Scripture and theology, was the possibility of grace. His was a tortured path to the recognition that faith demands action—in his case, to apply for conscientious objector status and leave the military.

This was not how he imagined his life would turn out. Born and raised in Iowa, in an evangelical Christian household, where he was taught to equate love of God with love of country, he signed up for the Army at the age of seventeen and won an appointment to West Point—only to drop out in his first term. Drifting from school to school (the University of Iowa, Colorado Christian University, the Colorado School of Mines), he studied literature and philosophy, wrote plays, and wrestled with issues like Christianity and patriotism, Just War and pacifism, truth and relativity—which informed his thinking when he returned to active duty in May 2002. Despite his misgivings about the war on terror, he entered the Defense Language Institute in Monterey, California, where he excelled in Arabic studies; his free time was taken up with matters of faith. Guided by the pronouncements of Rowan Williams, Archbishop of Canterbury, and Pope John Paul II, who condemned the invasion of Iraq, he began to articulate his opposition to the war, which in his view did not meet the definition of a Just War. Nevertheless he also became a gifted interrogator, and when he went to Abu Ghraib he was happy to employ his skills to elicit information from the Iraqis in his charge.

The interrogator and the prisoner: there is no more fraught relationship. For in this give-and-take any question, any answer, may determine an individual's fate. What better emblem of human conscience? In these pages we learn little of what actually occurred in Abu Ghraib—the messages were subject to military censorship—but we are privy to the self-examination of a man torn between the deception integral to his work and his Christian obligation to tell the truth. He is at once driven to excel and desperate to save his soul. He seems to have the makings of a charismatic leader or a monk. And if at the moment it seems that he is drawn toward the latter, awaiting a call to the priesthood, it is not difficult to imagine that more changes lie in his future.

The writings of the German Lutheran pastor and theologian Dietrich Bonhoeffer exerted a decisive influence on Casteel. Imprisoned by the Gestapo for his involvement in a plot to assassinate Hitler, Bonhoeffer used his time before he was hanged to compose a series of letters on the problem of becoming a Christian in our time, defining freedom in religious terms: "A prison cell, in which one waits, hopes—and is completely dependent on the fact that the door of freedom has to be opened from the outside, is not a bad picture of Advent." Freedom for him was thus a condition of his faith in the Risen Christ, a liberation that Casteel also experiences. The American soldier in Iraq, interrogating his own actions, recognizes, as Bonhoeffer wrote, that "Cheap grace is the mortal enemy of our church. Our struggle today is for costly grace." Such is the grace that Casteel knows.

This collection of email messages, the modern equivalent of the letter, is a record, not a reckoning; presumably the reckoning will come later, in more reflective writings. (Casteel is also a playwright and a memoirist.) Raw, guileless, this is the first draft of the history of an introspective young man. In a subsequent work perhaps he will reveal more about his assertion that his interrogations resulted in combat operations. Does he have the blood of innocents on his hands? Did this help to drive him out of the military? Answers to these questions must await another reckoning. For the book concludes with his conscientious objector hearing, where he made a speech that was the plea of a sinner praying for release—from the military and from the bonds of the self. "God help me," he pleaded.

What Joshua Casteel interrogates in *Letters from Abu Ghraib* is the very idea of liberty. For every enduring work of literature is an epistle from the prison of silence to the possibility of freedom. These cries from the heart will echo for a long time.

CHRISTOPHER MERRILL

PRE-DEPLOYMENT TO IRAQ

202nd *Military Intelligence Battalion*

FORT GORDON, GA

FROM ·······································JOSHUA
SENT ·····························05/04/2004 8:11 PM
TO ···PEARL
SUBJECT······································HEARING

So, I guess you've heard about the controversy at the prison in Iraq ... the abuse of Iraqi prisoners. It's been a strange past two days since I first heard. That's the same prison I'm heading to. A wave of feelings has rushed through me. Mostly contempt, bewilderment. The photos are horrific, and that's not what I was trained to do. I don't exactly know how to process this. For the most part, I know what the leadership of interrogation facilities do, and I've also heard that the military police (which is who the six perpetrators are) are not well educated in the Law of Land Warfare, or the Geneva Conventions (of which Interrogators have to be specialists). But when I hear the prisoners being called "detainees" it troubles me. Detainees have fewer rights than prisoners of war. POW's have special status as lawful combatants, heightening their Geneva Convention provisions. Since these prisoners are being labeled other than POWs, I don't know just how far envelopes are being pushed ... The angry side of me wants on the first plane,

3

and to be pinned my sergeant stripes as soon as possible so that
I can have some authority and ensure that nothing of the sort
happens under my watch. Then the "what the hell am I doing"
side of me shows up, wondering what a blond, blue-eyed Iowan
boy is doing in Iraq in the first place . . . at least with Caesar's
body armor and an M-16.

always,
joshua

THE JOINT INTERROGATION
AND DEBRIEFING CENTER

Abu Ghraib Prison

BAGHDAD, IRAQ

Hey, Mom. Yep, I live and work at the prison, both. The prison itself is quite huge, broken up into about eight sub-compounds, all about the size of medieval castles. There's actually more dust than sand, and dust covers everything. Palm trees peek up over the perimeter wall, and a few minarets. My "castle" has air conditioning and trailer-homes set up with showers and sinks. All onesies and twosies are done in porta-jons. I work in a compound about three football fields away, and eat and attend Mass at a compound about five football fields away. No Anglican chaplains, so I've been given another pastoral exception to attend Catholic Mass. There is an internet/telephone center and entertainment "shed" put on by Morale Welfare and Recreation (MWR) about two football fields away. Needless to say, getting around this place in 120-plus degree heat with 70 pounds of body armor and weaponry can be a bit taxing. I guess it helps me earn my meals, since the majority of my job here as an interrogator is intellectual (i.e., on my rear).

Today was my first day at the interrogation center, and my first impression was: I hate this job. But I worked through it and stayed on to get accustomed to my surroundings. I met the chaplain as well, he's Assemblies of God, and seems like a really great man. I told him I could sing, so I'm thinking he may have me do a special music sometime.

love,
joshua

FROM ···JOSHUA

SENT ·····························06/25/2004 9:34 AM

TO ··HOME

SUBJECT ··············RE: GLAD YOU MADE IT SAFELY

I guess now it's been about a week since I arrived to the Fertile Crescent, but for some reason it feels like it's been months. I left Fort Gordon, Georgia at about 10am eastern time, driving by charter bus to Atlanta.

Atlanta being our first "layover," although we had yet to fly anywhere, most of us were all anxiously looking forward to the traditional "two beers in transit" before taking off. But our Movement NCOIC (Non Commissioned Officer In Charge) SFC Smith spent three years as a basic training drill sergeant and he had no problem nixing our creature comforts. I, being pretty bent on having my beer, and making a little drama out of our "deprivation" ordered a St. Pauli's Girl non-alcoholic, and then invited SFC Smith to sit next to me. He gasped, thinking I'd simply ignored his order, but then laughed once he saw I'd ordered an NA.

After a two-hour layover in Germany, we re-boarded the plane and headed to Kuwait. I read my evening office of prayer from my newly received 1928 Book of Common Prayer/KJV Bible (thanks, Hannah!) and then continued in some reading of Hans Kung on the history of the Catholic Church. But that academic philosophical world of mine seemed to fade by the time I heard the captain state that we were flying over Baghdad. I looked out my window to see a patchwork of lights below, scattered loosely throughout the desert. And I forgot Professor Kung and his Church. One hour later we touched down in Kuwait.

The door to the plane opened to a pleasant warmth outside, which was surprising because I expected to be overtaken by blankets of heat. The short bus ride to Doha was littered with sporadic fires of oil fields in the distance, white clad wedding parties along roadsides, and sands which extended in all directions.

Once our names were finally called off on the flight manifest to head to Ali Al Saleem Airfield, we loaded another bus and headed toward the gate ... then the bus slowed to a halt. I heard a rather confused bus driver say "Mu aref, mu aref al tariq." Someone asked for a translator so I stepped to the front to figure out what had happened. As it turned out, our bus driver was one week on the job, just in from Turkey. And between the Arabic and Turkish I was able to make out, he knew just about nothing about just about everything in the area, not to mention that our US Army escort had been told just to show up to the bus, bring his weapon and ammo, and not to worry, "the drivers know where they are going."

So, with map in hand, I had to play navigator and interpreter all at once. "Well, let's get to it, you didn't learn Arabic for nothing," I told myself. And, after a rather bumpy "oh, we were supposed to take that exit" kind of ride, we finally arrived at Ali Al Saleem Airfield out in the Kuwaiti boonies. By this time I was pretty accustomed to the Middle Eastern heat, but when I realized that the 89 degree (F) tent we waited in felt completely frigid, I knew I wasn't in Kansas anymore.

We arrived to the Baghdad International Airport just shortly after sunrise and waited until early afternoon for the convoy which would take us to the Abu Ghraib prison, about 10 miles west of Baghdad. We were met by a three-vehicle convoy: one truck and two "gunships" (Hum-V's with 50cal machine guns mounted on top). We suited up in our body armor, Kevlar helmets, extra ammunition, etc., locked and loaded our M-16 rifles and received a briefing from the Army captain who told us of the current threat level, the history of past convoy ambushes, and that if we ever moved our M-16 selector levers from "safe" to "semi" automatic, we were to shoot to kill. My eyes were wide open on that drive, to say the least, and Toto and Auntie Em were nowhere to be found. Thanks be to God, we all made it safely to the prison, where I have begun my new existence.

I have been on the job at the interrogation center now for about five days, and I really love my work. I am not at liberty to discuss many details, but what I can say is that there are plenty of detainees here who are simply no joke. Some of the most unsavory of individuals committing indiscriminate acts (even against fellow Muslims) have passed through these walls. We released many detainees over the past three months (approx. 3 to 4 thousand), and with the ones remaining I play an integral role in getting to the bottom of incredibly heinous acts. And for those who are being held unjustly, I play an active role in their release, and can quite often form congenial relations with them (although actual friendships are obviously a little past the line of what is proper, or safe for the detainee).

Much has changed since the controversy, some for good and some for ill. Apart from the much-needed changes regarding detainee abuse, of which my colleagues know next to nothing, the knee-jerk reaction to ensure the world knows we obey the law has made things slightly difficult. There is a lot of discouragement on the part of interrogators, especially when known terrorists or criminals are across the table from us, and we are nearly impotent as to the level of surveillance authorized, authority to segregate/isolate, etc. There are those on Capital Hill who on the one hand desire "victory" in the "war on terror" and then on the other hand would have us just offer the terrorists tea and cigarettes to tell us where Bin Laden and Zarqawi are. This of course is absurd, being that Al Qaida operatives are trained to resist interrogation and to expect torture. Our "prison" probably seems like a resort. I'm not sure what is being reported in the US currently about Abu Ghraib, but conditions are pretty cush for our detainees.

13

I see my job much more as a Father Confessor than an interrogator. As a Confessor you cannot coerce a person to reveal that which they wish to hide. A Confessor's aim is to help the one confessing to be sincere, to arrive at the kind of contrition that actually desires self-disclosure—and to that end, empathy and understanding go a long way. No one actually wants secrecy, to carry the memory of shameful actions alone. A confessor provides the opportunity for a safe disclosure, offers a way out of secrecy. Interrogation is like a chess match, a battle of wits. But it is also a relationship of understanding, where I try to use a person's internal belief scheme to encourage them to narrate dishonorable actions with their own words. This tactic takes far more time and patience, but is far more effective in the long run and far more unsettling to the extremist Muslim who has been trained to prepare for torture. The aggressive approach reinforces their preconception that America is Satan and that the coalition is a Zionist conspiracy bent on their destruction. Empathy, if it is authentic itself, is incredibly unsettling, and forces a person to question the legitimacy of their training and indoctrination.

In many ways, I have no other recourse but to identify with these people. We spread democracy, and they are spreading the

Islamic State. And while we say that we are spreading the freedom of democracy, to so many of the Muslims in our wake, true freedom can only exist under the "rightful rule" of an Islamic Caliphate—much like the Jewish conception of the Messiah, or the millennial rule of Christ for Evangelicals. Our democratic freedom seems like nonsense ("grasping after the wind") to much of the Muslim world.

So, last night we were expecting a "planned attack" upon the prison . . . but, thanks be to God, I slept like a baby. Actually, I sleep more here than I have in a long, long time. By the time my workday ends, I'm simply beat. I rise at about 5am, work out and do the morning office of daily prayer, and then head to work. At lunch I've made a habit of eating with the local Iraqi workers, who are incredibly hospitable. There are always one or two 19 or 18 year-old uneducated Iraqis who are simply wide-eyed at my use of the Arabic language . . . "wait a minute, but you're white!" I come to the chapel at lunch and dinner to eat and pray, and I talk for a few minutes every lunch with Iraqis.

The Book of Common Prayer has become my blood and breath. I've also written a special rosary for personal concerns, which I pray about three times every day. There is morning and evening prayer with Scripture passages, and without this grounding I think I would have much more difficulty here. The scenery is incredibly desolate, the climate stifling, and the separation much more deep and compelling than when simply at a base in a state other than my home. A feeling of purpose and pride is real and aiding during my work day, but when I return to my room, sit on a bed and see my books and personal things, it's hard not to continue longing for the rest of my books, and, most importantly, for those close to me that I talk about these books with. Today was the first day I attended Mass, and thank God for that. The common prayers are somewhat depressing when I pray "we" and "our" alone in an empty chapel room.

On my first day on the job during initial training I had a severe sense of hopelessness and dread, not wanting to get into the interrogation process at all, wondering why I was not in school writing papers on philosophy and theology and preparing for the priesthood. But at the conclusion of training I read an article about Arab-American comparative psychology and I turned an about-face in a moment. Before I'd finished reading the introduction to the article, I'd become fascinated with my job, and authentically so. By the time I was given my leave to return to my room I had asked my supervisor if I could stay on after hours to read dossiers and more articles to get further acquainted with my surroundings. I can only attribute this instantaneous change to Grace and being lifted up in prayer, so thank you.

I continue on in my duties here, both to interrogate for the concerns of Iraqi-American security, and also for the mysterious purposes which have specifically brought me to this foreign land. And, as Father Confessor, I prayerfully continue forward. Pray for my comrades, who have quite clearly labeled me "the Chaplain" and for those for whom I will be their inquisitor. God grant me wisdom, compassion, and a genuine desire for Truth that knows no national patronage.

Another week at Abu Ghraib. Today is Friday. I woke about
9am and readied for Mass, walked across the compound and
arrived to the chapel just past 10am. But, due to increased re-
strictions on convoys (more attacks recently), the priest was
not able to come to the prison for Mass. It was pretty depressing. We have Protestant services on Sundays, both morning
and evening, which I will be able to attend this week since I
have Sunday off for the 4th of July. Thank God for that, but
keeping the liturgy with others and taking the Eucharist—
Communion—is the most important part of the week for me.
So, I found a candle, lit it upon the altar, prayed my Rosary and
then proceeded to do the liturgy and Scripture readings by myself. I was glad to be able to offer this service in the absence of
the priest, as the prayers and readings still needed to be said
with or without the priest, but the absence of the Eucharist
was difficult. I sat in the chapel, reading and praying, for about
45 minutes and when I reached the end, I simply sat with my

Bible and Prayer Book in hand, pressed to my forehead, not wanting to leave—wanting to stay in the comfort of a Church, even if only constructed impromptu, and congregated only by myself and the Holy Spirit.

Last Sunday I attended evening Protestant services and lost my voice singing. I stayed to pray, mostly on account of my duties as an interrogator. The weight of the job sometimes is more painfully present to me than other times. Sometimes the lies I hear from detainees are easily distinguishable from the truth, but at other times they are not so easy to discern. And, while I understand quite clearly the role of judgment and wielding authority for the punishment/prevention of crime in society, this is a duty I assume with no joy. I do so because it is what has been asked of me, and I continue to do so with the greatest amount of integrity I can muster. But how I would much rather speak of Grace with those across my table, and tell them of the alternative to their chosen path. And, for as long as I sit in my current seat of authority, with a weapon strapped across my back, the moral high ground seems somewhat clouded.

While praying that Sunday, I pleaded for a reason or insight into my current role that would help me see more clearly. The very next thing I saw in my mind was the turning of the tables of the money lenders in the temple—Christ calling them a den of robbers, a brood of vipers. I am quite sure that Christ sympathized with their circumstances, the Israelite and Palestinian country tradesmen in Roman-occupied Jerusalem. But understanding and sympathy themselves do not equate to moral tolerance: action and accountability were still required of the tradesmen who were turning the temple into a strip mall. Similarly might I sympathize with the disenfranchised of this country being taken advantage of by the foreigners flocking to Baghdad, Fallujah and Mosul. But something must be done to show the grave consequences of these choices. I most commonly do this by attempting to speak with them on their level —get to know them, understand where they come from, their families, and show them the futility of their violent choices. But every time I kneel before the cross, praying both for them and more so for me, I ask God to give me the time when I might put down my own sword, put down this seat of authority, and pick up the Eucharist. How much I would rather be a priest to these men than their accuser.

Monday or Tuesday we received mortars at about 9pm. I was helping my roommate sling his weapon when a big crash rumbled somewhere in the compound. I asked him if he heard it, and he replied coolly, "yeah, we're being attacked." And then we continued about our business. The casualness of it all was pretty humorous. I was just getting ready to go to the shower trailers to get ready for bed when the mortars came in, so I had to nix that for the evening. Minor inconvenience, I guess, in exchange for my safety.

Yesterday, more mortars came down on other bases in the Baghdad area. At lunch, a troop of Marine engineers came to clear a minefield outside the interrogation facility, and once we were given the "all-clear" sign to go outside, I ran post haste to a porta-jon, being that we'd been locked-down for about two hours! While in the jon I heard another boom, which I later learned had been an improvised explosive device (IED) that had gone off on one of our convoys 160 meters from the prison ... but was still powerful enough to shake the building (and my porta). I haven't heard anything about the convoy, injuries or other. We basically take no news as good news. But, due to things like this, we haven't received any mail convoys or priests.

Today I sat down in the dining hall with two of my Iraqi friends and discussed the current state of Iraq in Arabic. My ears are still pretty shoddy after a rifle qualification course back at Fort Gordon—I forgot to use hearing protection on a timed qual-course and 20 rounds of m-16 fire went off inches from my ears. It makes hearing in crowded places kind of difficult. But we were still able to have a pretty good conversation. The everyday Iraqi, in the opinion of these men, simply doesn't care about politics, democracy, Islamic Caliphates, pan-Arabism or other idealistic concepts. They want electricity, running water and food on their tables for their children. They want whatever can provide for their basic necessities, and if America and the coalition can bring that to them, great. If not, "who can?" is their basic question. Pretty reasonable, I think.

Baghdad has the bad luck of having received the first installment of amenities, which it had to part with as the coalition tried to extend facilities more evenly throughout the rest of the country. So electricity is about 40% less available in Baghdad now than four or six months ago. Numbers change all the time, and sentiment changes with them. Ideas, Western or Islamic or other, don't have as much sway, though, as do the basic needs of fathers to put food on the table. Please pray for these needs, much more than for my own. I have my needs met, and a great many of my desires, even. Humanitarian assistance is

our best weapon against terrorism—give the terrorists no social or economic foothold into the weaknesses of the poor. We
don't have to export and expand America (or Democracy even)
to places of fear and struggle. I truly believe we simply have to
but offer out of our abundance to those who have little. Snub
the skepticism of those who fear we will be another imperial-
ist benchmark in the history of Middle Eastern colonialism.
Extremists are the minority, but skepticism and contempt for
the West is widespread. Our fight cannot be against flesh and
blood, but against doubt, against mistrust, against fraud, and
against manipulation.

Today was interesting ... my two big interrogations ... and they went very well. But, more challenges with my work. Subtleties, I'd say, for sure, but things that are important for me. You must pardon me, as figuring out what may be said and what must be kept silent goes through the ever annoying filter of "national security." I really hate secrets. To put it vaguely, it's the strategy games I have to play with the man across the table from me, mixing and meshing shades of truth and lies to assess his responses and defense mechanisms, from which I write my reports and gather information. So much hinges upon my instincts, and when it matters, I'd say I'm pretty damn good at what I do ... which is, in itself, a little frightening. We use the term "exploitation" very casually—as in, exploit as much information of intelligence value in the least amount of time possible. It always takes time, and the only shortcuts come when an interrogator outsmarts his or her detainee. But it's all such a dance: motives, methods, means, and then what you do with what you get, and how much you trust those who then do what they do with what you give them. It can be quite paralyzing.

We're nowhere near anything "controversial," because my moral dilemma is miles within the bounds of what CNN and the BBC care about . . . I just think I'm called to something nobler, which means I have to spend more energy wrestling through the issues of detainee treatment. I'm going to see how much of this I can talk over with a Catholic chaplain. I don't really want to go to the Evangelical pastors because I fear they will be too easily swayed by the necessity to wage strategies with combatants . . . and Catholics are usually much more fervent and consistent than Protestants in not bowing blindly to the State (they've kind of got their own polis over there in Rome). Perhaps I'll be able to call soon.

I love you,
joshua

FROM ·· JOSHUA

SENT ···························· 07/14/2004 12:35 AM

TO ·· FM

SUBJECT ···················· TRIAL AND PERSEVERANCE

Hey, Father M, how are you? How's St. John's? The Crew team? Life here in Iraq continues, I've been reading a lot from Pope John Paul II and Thomas Merton, have kept the daily offices without fail since my arrival, but, all in all, my spiritual life here has transformed in a way I did not anticipate. I have encountered a different kind of dependence: the spiritual disciplines, in their traditional sense of liturgical prayer, meditation, scripture readings, etc., have such a prominent place in my life now. The feeling of necessity, what feels totally amiss in the world if I have not observed these disciplines, has been the most new—startling even. In that sense, I feel so much more grounded spiritually than I ever have, or at least this spiritual place is so very different than the intuitive spirituality I have typically known and lived out. Quite often I even avoid my own words in prayer, intentionally so as to avoid self-formation. Rather, my hope is to be shaped by the prayers of the liturgy and psalms, and this seems to be happening in my attitudes and in my desires. I know that my circumstances have directly resulted in this dependency, for which I have nothing but thanks that God will continue to send me to the places that will force me to see beyond myself. But the weight of this job is increasingly difficult. More than anything, I ask that you would pray for me.

Being a man's inquisitor in the name of a secular justice feels so often like fraud. Usually the day can be managed, and I try simply to focus on my own integrity and to hear what the Spirit is speaking to me in the midst of my interrogations, but I fight continually to try to see what is behind this political facade; to see why I have been sent here for this mission at this point in time, and how I am to respond to it, how God wishes to test me and unveil His plan in and through me. Many people here, Christians and non- alike, try to remind me that "they are the enemy" or that these people are "the instruments of Satan" and that I am dispensing the judgment they are due. And, to a degree, they are right. But I cannot help but believe that I have no enemies (only "lawful combatants") and that the belief that I am opposing "the instruments of Satan" and am hence justified to antagonize them brings me dangerously close to the fundamentalism we ourselves are fighting.

I understand the role of the sword in governments is to punish vice, but to confuse that with "Justice" is naive at best, and to actually desire to wield that sword is increasingly becoming something beyond my ability. If God bids me stay, I shall, and I will continue to find whatever ways are available to me to Christianize this endeavor and conduct my duties with integrity. As things have progressed thus far, I have had and continue to have so very many opportunities to serve and share Christ. One of my Air Force friends who is a carpenter just made for me a portable kneeler so that I don't bruise my knees while keeping the liturgy. God will show me a way as I continue to pray for the strength and courage to be faithful to it. But it is hard, and so very often all I wish to do is to drop my weapon, walk out the gates, and take my bloated military paycheck with all its wartime additions and start helping the impoverished people out in Baghdad who, if not utterly confused and desperate, would probably be living quite simple lives rather than being manipulated by both the rich Islamists and Western Democratists vying for their moral and material allegiance. Nobody seems willing to fight for these people simply for these people's own benefit, apart from what it will gain either the future caliphate or Western alliances. Well, I've continued on long enough.

love,
joshua

As always, Father, God has majestically endowed you with an inviolable thirst for honesty . . . even amidst the briars on your path. I think it is Romans 8 where St. Paul continues on about doing that which he desireth not, or, the eternal struggle for authenticity incumbent upon us all. That passion is fanned and tempered, weathered and tested, and once the stillness closes in about, the flame is given breath to grow. I will pray and continue to do so, for the monastery, for the stillness you desire. In some ways, this place has become my monastery. I remain quiet in the evenings and read incessantly, mostly with a heart of sorrow. I attend Protestant chapel and engage with them when energy permits, but the kind of rejoicing in worship which they attempt to draw out of people is very difficult for me. It is not that I have nothing in which to rejoice, but my posture of expression is one on my knees, or my forehead pressed upon the prayer book. Silence is one of the only ways I know to deal with this madness. And that is simply what it is, madness. I just interrogated a man who without doubt deserves, by any reasonable standard, what awaits him, in this world and the next. One might think me justified then in being his accuser, the role of which I certainly play, and with no small amount of animation. But there is a line in the movie The Cardinal where Father Steven tells his archbishop that he feels he cannot be a priest because when people unveil their sins to him in confession, it is they who confess and yet he who trembles. He understands and loves the law, but he is terrified at being the one who dispenses it. I simply pray that God teaches me with clarity where I must go—shows me real Justice and how to be its ambassador, grants me grace and shows me how not to fear to receive it, leads me toward the cross and grants me the courage to bear it. That kind of honesty is the only hope for a Church blind to its own needs.

love always,
joshua

The parched desert air wraps around your face and hands like a stale blanket. Foot and vehicle prints can almost never be traced from one day to the next, the wind blowing yesterday's treads into the air. This is the path I just took. That is where I just stepped. But the gash in the earth that yesterday laid open, has been filled tomorrow by dirt and shovels, erasing the land with a newness of cables and wires, stone and steel.

Walking through the many courtyards, Arabic numbers tattoo the walls—sayings and drawings and proverbs on the inner perimeter. Al mustuqbul li'nah, wa lay'sa li'eaudi'unah: "The future is for us, and not for our enemies." A patchwork of punctured brick backdrops the ascension of 1 to 10 written on a courtyard wall, on the other side of which prisoners once lived in barred cells. I wonder what events there, too, the winds and workmen's hands now seek to erase from memory. Their voices are not heard, but I feel as if they walk beneath my treads and linger on beneath me as I walk daily upon the dirt, which I breathe into my lungs.

At the prison's edge is a teetering skyline—minaret, palm trees, the mosaic dome of a mosque, rooftops. At sunset I can hear the calls to prayer from the south and from the east. At times it may even appear as if in a round, like choirs of a cathedral, one folded atop the other. But always a few hours after the sun has fallen there is the intermittent echo of small-arms fire, the howling of dogs. Today the earth is carved by the claws of 210mm artillery rounds hidden in the back of a stolen vehicle parked on the road near an American checkpoint. Tomorrow, buildings and roads, pipes and electrical wires, bandaging and suturing what's already been forgotten.

From the rising to the setting of the day's enveloping heat the droning hums and vibrations of wheels, machines and wind follow my steps and cover my ears. It is impossible to listen amongst the ever-present chatter of inanimate voices. The days merge one to the next and bear no distinction from one to the other—for the same conversation marks them all, tireless wind and ever-laboring generators. Memory itself seems forgotten amidst the ever forward-pressing sameness.

I cannot tell the men across my table what I pray in solitude. I cannot tell them except what their ears will hear, and yet in hearing, they do not understand, for Doubt is their lord and comforter. Inside this captivity I cannot forgive what is not confessed, and thus so many must retain what I cannot absolve. God forgive me for those whose yokes I cannot carry. Forgive me for the stories I cannot see behind fig ruses. Forgive me Lord if my own atonement is incomplete, and for this imperfect justice that sends me to them, yearning to be Your Minister.

I woke up a few days ago in a puddle. The generators, which I wrote spin tirelessly for our livelihood, failed at my compound. It was a pretty tragic series of days. In case you don't know exactly what a generator failure means, our many (and quite needed!) A/C units have these little umbilical chords attaching them to our mother and life source (electricity), by which they derive their life and being. Praise be to God, from whom all blessings of conditioned air do flow, I no longer have to grow gills in order to sleep through the night. That, and it would have been only a matter of time before my batteries would have been exhausted, and flashlights are only tolerable for so long. I guess, though, these kinds of inconveniences connect me a little more viscerally to the many (so very, very many) war fighters having to battle the heat in direct sunlight day after day.

Some good news came in today. Special requirements came down my way concerning a detainee I've been questioning.

Well, I was just notified that the results of my past three interrogations received special recognition from "higher up." I guess my cigarettes and smiles with the ruthless man I spoke briefly of earlier did something profitable for the commanders in the field. That was a big boost of confidence, being that the best thing I did was simply respect him, and talk to him as if I had no idea of his past crimes—which, in as much as I can disclose, were simply unbelievable—and apparently, valuable information was gleaned. Listening goes so much further than speaking, generally. People usually broadcast their lies and anxieties by what they say or fail to say. If one is patient enough to listen, criminal guilt or shame in general will show itself, unless a person is an actor or pathological. I imagine this is simply the natural corollary to "what is done in the dark, will be seen in the light." Listening to the cues of a person who does not want to come right out and say something, but doesn't want to continue carrying a burden of guilt or shame, is not only what interrogation is about . . . it's what being a decent human being is about. I do not coerce. I cannot say that emphatically enough. Not emotionally, not psychologically, and certainly not physically. Everyone, however, has some level of desire to be understood, and to be justified in their actions or beliefs. Knowing the other person, understanding them in their own convictions, and listening to them tell their own stories is something I value (and, apparently, now so do the "higher ups"). I think this is God's answer to prayer, a little bit of sense in this madness I'm a part of here.

Foreigners (extremists from Syria, Saudi Arabia, Jordan, Yemen) use the lack of education, lack of jobs, and extreme poverty (due to the 13 years of economic sanctions) to enlist broken-spirited Muslims into terrorist or other anti-coalition groups and activities. When faced with the options of remaining under Saddam, or listening to what simply has to appear to them like another big-money rich white aristocrat from the West (interested in them for their business prospects and political capital), or another Muslim who looks and talks like them . . . what kind of choices do these people have? 500 years of previous colonialism. 40-some years under Saddam. 13 years of not being able to buy penicillin or pencils, because they were banned under the embargo (as "weapons materials"). Or perhaps a war with another man named Bush who told the Shia and the Kurds to rise up in revolt against Saddam and we'd support them . . . only to have them meet a massacre when we did not support this uprising.

And amazingly, the vast majority desperately wanted the Americans to come ... basically, to finish what they started 13 years ago. But the change, both which we promised and they so desperately desired, has not come. And how could it? We are an Army equipped to fight an enemy, but that means knowing who that enemy is. The once-"soldiers" (of the old Iraqi Army) became "terrorists" in the war on terror, became "insurgents" in the reconstruction, and are now in some cases becoming "allies" in nation building. How could they be expected to believe us? Previously, when people opposed Saddam, their entire families would be summarily executed. When Western nations came to these lands in the past, it was for one reason: to create colonies of a far-off empire. There is a line in The Patriot when General Cornwallis tells his commander to pipe down his own terror tactics, because "after this war, we will re-establish commerce with these people, we cannot make enemies with them" or something to that effect. These people have known colonialists and totalitarians also. And now, a Texan oil tycoon from the land of opportunity (with the most destructive army in the history of warfare) tells them they are free.

There is such a toll on the hearts of Americans as well. Soldiers want something to believe in, a cause bigger than themselves to make sense of it all, and they'll often grow cold toward the Iraqis. "Why don't they understand, show us some appreciation? I'm risking my life for them." It's just not that simple. In so many ways, this just has to be a thankless job—maybe something hard for a 19 year-old Marine to understand. The Iraqis don't have the luxury to "trust" our good intentions, they've been taken advantage of for all of modern history. There simply is not the precedent to warrant that kind of faith, let alone faith in a foreign power. Trust extends to the edges of the tribe, everyone else is someone who might turn you in to the Fedayeen Saddam, a Gestapo-like organization made for civic domination. And then when their sister, cousin, brother is killed in a well-intentioned precision guided bomb that goes off-course, destroying a housing complex, you can't tell them, "We meant well."

I've reconnected with my Iraqi friend Lazim, who works with the coalition, after weeks of conflicting lunch schedules and a dining facility change of location. We've been talking about the Koran and the Bible, Jesus and the Virgin Mary, Shias, Sunnis, Catholics, Protestants, and . . . computers. He's been wanting to get a laptop for a while and has enough money to spend about $700 (contracted local nationals get paid pretty good wages). Well, I've found a fully equipped, DVD and all, laptop online that we're looking to order for him. Only, I'd like to see about getting it without him paying for it. I'm prepared to front a good amount, if not all, but if anyone would like to be a part of this computer purchase, let me know. I try to talk to locals as much as I possibly can, if only "good morning" in Arabic, or thanking them for their hard work, which is often incredibly difficult manual labor. I'm glad I can do this, being that not many here know Arabic, but I'd love to be able to do a bit more than just offer courtesy of tongue.

love always,
joshua

Hot off the wire.

I got into a bit of a dinner-time tussle with a guy in my unit last night. I read a quote by Donald Rumsfeld: "I do not foresee extending the tours of Guard and Reserve Units to longer than 24 months, but one should never say never...the situation on the ground will determine that." Well, I was of the opinion that this statement was incredibly arrogant and bullheaded. I interpreted it as, "I don't ever have to re-assess my policy decisions, because everything I do is simply an accurate and appropriate reaction to the way things are in reality." To extend the tours of Reserve forces beyond what even Regular Army forces conduct is preposterous. Troops are not chess pieces. And Reservists have other lives. Well, my friend didn't like the idea of a man in uniform criticizing the Secretary of Defense. I did in fact go too far when I said he was a "shitty war planner." But I was not going to just roll over because some bully

41

can't argue coherently on his own. So, I went to the appropriate army regulation (AR 600-20, para 5-3 and appendices B and C) to vindicate the rights of enlisted service members to hold and express political opinions as long as they are not doing so as a representative of the US Army, or using undue command influence over subordinate troops. The idea that I was just going to hush up, or in the words of not a few Marines and infantrymen "shut the fuck up, do your job!" wasn't gonna fly, and I'm not going to kowtow to intimidation. If I can be simply shut up by bullies who can't think coherently, or if the Army is allowed to use such bullies to chill civil discourse, then democracy does not work, it has not been achieved, and everything we say we are doing here is worthless and a lie. But, contrary to the popular opinion that intellectuals don't get their hands dirty, I'm "doing my job" every (add expletive of choice with gusto) day. Someone else's intellectual or emotional insecurity, or inability to discipline themselves in the midst of intellectual critique, is not my problem.

I love you.
joshua

Well, today is my day off. I'm watching The Mission with my friend Tom (eh-hem, SGT Winisko, that is), who is the ranking interrogator on our two-man team. Last night I also watched for the second time the PBS Frontline special on Pope John Paul II. Dad, I almost started crying five minutes into the movie, but there were two other guys in the room playing video games and listening to horrid music on the other side of my earphones. Hearing stories of his childhood—his success as a goalie in soccer, his acting, his poetry, the comments of the young women around him when he was a young priest who said that he was "fully a man, but not like a man looking for girlfriends . . . but he was fully a man" . . . it excites me, Dad. When I see the opening scenes of The Mission and I see three Jesuit priests walking through the jungles of South America, with no possessions, nothing tying them down, except for the Church in whose service they have given their lives entirely (and practically, not just metaphorically), I just want to jump up and down.

43

Dad, I don't want a life of possessions. I don't want a life filled with the many addictions and allegiances of civic life. I don't want to be a Democrat. I don't want to be a Republican. I don't want to be an American, if that means forming my convictions and beliefs in accordance with something as mundane as dirt and committees and geopolitical interests. I belong to none of them. Moreover, I believe the Church was intended as a sign of the world to come, something which human government cannot attain. I don't want to politic between the social justice of the Democrats and the personalist morality of the Republicans, neither of which have any tangible authority over issues of God and Truth. I want to speak with authority from a position of authority, one ordained by God. I want to submit to an authority that is not of myself, and I want to authentically "abandon all" in the proper way which maintains Pauline love, and does not evade life's issues for the wrong reasons. How shall I use my talents? I want to know what will most profit the Church, beyond Rome, beyond Canterbury, beyond Constantinople, and beyond the many American assemblies. How am I to be in Her service?

Freedom is not bought by pipelines being made in Afghanistan, nor by the major private corporations handling construction and oil distributions (Enron, Halliburton) who profit incredibly by the joint military venture/tax breaks set forth by the Bush Administration. Freedom is not made behind closed doors with Saudi regimes (who espouse the very same Wahabist Sunni ideas as the terrorists) because we fear losing their input in the American economy (which is over 7%). My contention with George Bush is not one of believing him malevolent, but rather believing him unwise and guilty of maligning God's freedom with mere political rhetoric. Political freedom certainly involves a whole lot of this "dirty work" because political freedom is a perversion of freedom, and it is an exclusive freedom which can only be offered to those who are the same as those offering it—we can only "liberate" a people by making them like us. Spiritual freedom is similar, it involves conversion. But spiritual conversion is optional, freely offered, freely rejected, and the converted are called to love the unconverted, not bend them to their will by, say, "regime change" of the inner person.

It is a myth and an illusion to suppose that political freedoms can ascend to the level of the Gospel—it is also a form of blasphemy and idolatry. The more Christianity joins the moralistic banter of neo-conservative Republican-Christianity, the more democracy is de-legitimized, the more the Gospel is profaned, and the more we bow ourselves to a second master—one clad as an angel of light.

There must be examples, and a growing culture that is itself this example, of the freedom which Christ instituted, not which was allegedly given at Plymouth Rock and written about in Adam Smith's "The Wealth of Nations." Nationalistic myths are what convince peoples to take up the sword. Yes, I think that we should "take a little wine" for our stomachs, and not disdain the wisdom which is inscribed in nature for our survival and edification (i.e., modern medicine). Yes, I think that we should promote democracy and not disdain the offerings, be they imperfect, of political bodies. But Capital Hill has replaced the Vatican, and hospitals and political parties have replaced the Church as the "new salvation," granting "life" and "freedom" to those who follow their teaching. We don't need the Eucharist, we have medicine. Democracy is now forced upon peoples like Christianity was during the Holy Roman Empire, in the "Christianizing" of civilization—now, we're "Democratizing," and instead of the Pope or an Emperor, we have the American President. I do think that we should encourage those systems of government which most allow people to freely choose, especially with regard to religion. But there are subtle concessions being made, Dad, concessions I don't want to allow in my life. I do not want to confuse the hope of God with the hope of men, nor the promises of God with the promises of men. I greatly fear that the future of the Gospel is at stake in these confusions—what do we tell the people who do not hear the Gospel, but hear the promises and pledges of society day in and day out, seeing also the continued injustices witnessed on television and in the news?

love,
joshua

Our battle is not one of flesh and blood, but of spiritual powers and principalities. When evil is identified in men/things
and we destroy creatures/creations, redemption is nullified
and significance forgotten in our inability to see beyond the
mere sign. When an evil is committed and the perpetrator
killed, the evil (the significance) does not die, only the sign, the
creature. To kill evil one must kill the significance, which can
only come through conversion, through an internal transformation of Being, what theologians call "redemption"—which
is simply the recollection that creation is good. That is the task
of righteousness, to overcome evil by remembering that Being
is Good. Evil is never eliminated, goodness is simply remembered. Goodness, the significance of the Creator, cannot be
destroyed—thus, neither can evil. Goodness can be forgotten,
perverted, or misused, but never destroyed. When an "evil
man" is killed, it is only the sign, the creation which dies—not
the evil. Goodness is procreative, not destructive. It is when

goodness is forgotten or abandoned that evil is given reign. The reign of evil is the failure of creation to walk in the fullness of simply having been created—created in the image of a Creator who only creates good. Goodness is simply the effect of having been created by the Creator, thereby enabled to be procreative rather than destructive. Realizing this connection is the pivotal point in further "creation of good."

FROM ·JOSHUA

SENT· ·08/08/2004 1:44 AM

TO ·ALL

SUBJECT ·RE: FW: FROM JOSH

So, here's my first draft of why prayer has been so hard for me recently.

I'm simply livid. I walk around the prison so often wanting to hit things, or scream. I just want to step into the Oval Office and scream some release.

You can't call this man "Pro-Life"—look at the countless lives devastated by 13 years of economic sanctions, followed by a "shock and awe" campaign that left Baghdad in shambles, followed by a quick-fix sugar high of economic progress as the regime fell, which ultimately gave way to the utter joblessness that ensued, followed by the occupation, raids and chopper attacks that kill WTF-ed dumbfounded Iraqis, sometimes in numbers as high as 300!!!

Campaigning in the name of Life and Family in circumstances such as these, to my mind, is simply unconscionable. And if I could sit down with the commander in chief right now, and talk things through, I too would simply say "shame on you, Mr. Bush." How dare you take up the sword Peter was told to lay down, and use it in the name of a freedom which cannot be won by force. Is Bush "Pro-Family" for all the Reservists and National Guardsmen valiantly fighting for a commander who tells them they must do the job of Regular military personnel for two entire years!! How dare you waste our human and natural resources on a war of convenience (not necessity) that inhibits our abilities to fight the groups that are actually responsible for the attacks in memory of which we marched off in the first place. Where's Al Qaida? Where's Bin Laden? Where is the investigation into the nation from which all of the 9-11 hijackers were natural-born citizens (Saudi Arabia). No, a nation so strangled by sanctions that it could not import pencils or penicillin somehow had a WMD infrastructure so advanced that it could attack the US or her Allies in 30 minutes time? And we want to give this man the reward of a second term?

The entire country should drop to its knees. But maybe I have no ground to rest on because I myself cannot. Just crawl out of Abu Ghraib on my knees. Maybe my anger is blinding my arrogance.

love,
joshua

Mom/Dad,

I'm so very angry right now, I'm not sure where to begin.

Mom, I can understand if, by means of argument, you disagree with me, and you have x,y, and z reasons as to why you think this or that of what I am saying is wrong, naive, misfounded, whatever. But to say that you think my ideological problems may be the result of not properly dealing with emotional stress, or my "circumstance," is simply below the belt.

I do not understand why the two of you cannot apply your marriage/family counseling wisdom to cultures and societies. Defense mechanisms, vulnerability, communication, servanthood, leadership—why is it you cannot see these dynamics between nations?

Why is everything seen through the lens of patronage and "teams." If I criticize a group, say, Republicans, for this or that policy, somehow that translates for you as, "The Democrats have it right." Dad, when you criticize or challenge a husband for not engaging his wife, for not drawing her out, does that mean that the wife has been perfect? And that to solve the problem, the husband must now kowtow to the wife? Of course not!

For the love of God, why is criticism of the war on Iraq (from personal experience, mind you)—and even a sincere desire for Bush to get ousted come November—a statement that he has been hatching the demise of innocent Iraqis and John Kerry is the Messiah? If Bush gets us into preventable wars, and propounds intelligence that's laughable, and, to my opinion, is sowing the seeds of a FUTURE jihad against western civilization because he is culturally INEPT, I think it within the bounds of sound reason to say, "You know what, maybe we oughtta look around for a replacement."

I talk to Iraqi farmers and taxi drivers who simply never would've been mixed up in terrorism or other violence if we hadn't blown up their cousins and apartments with precision guided bombs! THAT WAS NOT A NECESSARY DEATH! Bush might have a great personal faith in Jesus Christ, but his public application of that faith is deplorable, and the militant way in which conservative American Christians naively "support the troops" makes me sick. We are not saving the massacre of 6 million Jews. We are not opposing the immanent destruction of Western Liberal Democracies, even though this is what we are being told. We are sending the Marines and Special Forces after 30-year-old fathers of four who are so damn desperate to put food on the table that they will listen to seductive traps from rich Saudi and Syrian militants offering them kinship, protection, and provision. And when someone of the same religion, heritage, and color of skin comes to you, shakes your hand and calls you brother, it's a little more believable than when a rich white Christian who made a fortune in oil just booms into your town with tanks and choppers talking of "freedom" and "liberation" a year after he talked of "Operation Infinite Justice" (the first name for the war on terrorism) as a "crusade" against terror. It took priests and rabbis to tell Bush he could not call a military campaign "infinitely just," because, as he may have forgotten, only God is infinitely just ... and, don't you think that the nation's foremost diplomat, in an attempt to build a coalition of nations, might not want to use the word "crusade" when trying to get Arab (MUSLIM!!!) nations to help?

You're right, Mom. This is not a simple issue . . . it is incredibly complex. This administration has been tunnel-visioned about Iraq. Report after report after report (going all the way back to the original Iraq strategy in 2000–2001 published on the website of the Project for the New American Century) confirms that Iraq was a priority almost immediately after 9-11. Report after report after report continues to confirm that in all likelihood, Saddam probably DID get rid of his stockpiles (something inspectors kept on trying to tell the administration, but they would not listen).

I can't avoid politics here, I AM the front lines of US foreign policy. People tell me what happened to their kids and cousins during the embargo, how their hopes were dashed after an economic spike that gave way to joblessness. I have to listen to the US soldiers mock Iraqis among themselves, saying how they hate this country and these people because they are simply too afraid to say that they don't understand why they are here. I have to doubt every word detainees say to me (if I'm not to be laughed at by my colleagues), when more often than not, I'm skeptical of the crappy reporting being done by our Iraqi contacts (not to mention the CIA), and the corruption of Iraqi police (not to mention US Special Forces), turning in innocent people for bribes so that they can create "good relations" (translation: $$$) with the units glad to finally "get a bad guy." I simply cannot believe the mess we've created here . . . not that I'm going to give up, we have to press on and make up for our failings. But we cannot continue on blindly as if nothing wrong ever happened.

I'm sorry for being so emotional about this, it's what I live in day and night . . . and all the while I have to ask myself, "How should I then live?" Read the sermon on the mount, say the morning and evening liturgy, attempt to think that Christianity is greater than sock puppet stories and a bunch of principles that apply only when nothing's at stake . . . and then try to do my job for a day. Again, forgive my impertinence.

love,
joshua

FROM ···JOSHUA

SENT ·······························08/13/2004 11:31 PM

TO ···ALL

SUBJECT ························RE: PART V, IN PART . . .

My roommates almost got into a violent fight this evening. And it started over an incredibly important controversy: whether the Chevy or the Ford pickup truck is more likely to rust. E says, "I don't even let my dad mouth off to me like that, I'm not gonna let you." C, afraid and rather defeated says, "I'm just tired of you telling me to shut the f up all the time...I'd just like it if you'd talk to me with a little respect." At first I was stunned and motionless in my chair. I hadn't expected E to explode like he did, and over something so utterly meaningless. Feeling C pummeled by both words and (nearly) fists, though, I stepped in and let E know he sounded like a frightened boy, not a capable man commanding respect. E was handling a knife (something actually quite common) as he paced around the room a bit. I backed off. E fell asleep. C lay in bed, stunned from the emotional blow, too humiliated to say again that he'd been hurt.

All the while I was reading a small book by Henri Nouwen, with chapter headings like "Do You Love Me?" and "From Relevance To Prayer." I felt a conundrum, to say the least. I wanted to jump to my feet, further exacerbate the pain E had inherited from his father (previous conversations) and make him feel helpless and weak once more, but this time in the presence not of his father, but of C. Not on my watch, I said inside, not while C is being walked over by an insecure boy in man's clothing.

Every day I wonder if I have reached my limit. Every day I wonder if I have come to my breaking point. How can I continue in this matrix of power and the will to power? Why is it I have come at all, if only to say I cannot? And yet something stays me where I stand. Is it courage or is it cowardice? I hear the reports come back about the "relevance" of my intelligence gathering in the field, but feel like the 18-year-old kid who watched a courtyard of US Army cadets form a sea of gray and white from the rear view mirror of my taxi car. Do I now drop out of West Point here, too?

Today I was counseled concerning my upcoming promotion to Sergeant. My chain of command will be helping me assemble my various parcels for the promotion packet to go before the promotion board in a month or so. Making Sergeant was the one thing I had as a goal in my enlistment. I wanted the leader's post of a working man, to earn my stripes and my respect from a job well done, earned by exertion, not by my college success. My section leader challenged me as to whether I could give instructions and orders that conflicted with my personal morality. I instinctively said that if asked by subordinates I would tell exactly where I stood morally on any position, but that I would delineate between what is legal/doctrinal and what is the gray-shaded moral landscape within those boundaries. He was concerned about how I could lead others as interrogators while not binding them with my personal moral ethic. My response— separate church and state.

How is that the way? How can I lead people in the will to power? Being who I am? Is it not absolutely contrary to everything central to the Kingdom of the New Testament? How can I accept this post? How can I willingly offer myself to it? How can I even begin to offer guidance in an area I feel so utterly lost in as it is? I'm no longer the same 18 year-old that once wore a cadet's gray uniform.

God forgive our lack of faith, our unwillingness to believe in Your redemption, and our efforts to conjure our own. We die of self-absorption, convinced of our own myths of importance. Forgive my conflicting allegiances and doubt.

love,
joshua

Dad,

I find it at least ironic that whenever Christians make biblical references in support of war sentiments, it is by means of the Old Testament. Have we forgotten that God said it was an evil desire leading Israel to establish a King? And "Thou shall not kill"? And "Vengeance is mine, sayeth the Lord"? When Christ spoke the beatitudes, he stood on a hill high above a Palestinian peasantry, ruled by a Hasmonean ruler of the Roman Empire, Herod. The opulence of this society, sexually and politically, had ravaged the resources of the disenfranchised, had raped her women, had placed statues in the holy of holies, all in the wake of Alexander the Great's profane and bloody conquests of the ancient Mediterranean and beyond. And it was to THIS people that Christ said, "turn the other cheek." Christ stood above this peasantry and said not only is adultery wrong, but lust is just as evil. Not only is killing wrong, but hate, even calling your friend a "moron" endangers you of hell fire. If a man strikes you, turn to him your other cheek. If somebody wants to borrow from you, never withhold from him, and if he wants you to travel to Jerusalem, go with him all the way to Antioch. In their hearts, they must have laughed him off the hill. "Tell that to the centurion who just raped my sister and axed my cousin!" We laugh him off the hill now, too. When are we going to take his words seriously? Or will we resort to the same old verses, and come up with, say, reasons it's good to forfeit our virgin daughters to evil men, simply because Lot did it in Sodom?

love,
joshua

Was Rome dispensing "God's divine Justice" when it forbade Peter and Paul from preaching in public? Were Peter and Paul "justly reprimanded for their sins" by being imprisoned and executed? Was Jesus being justly punished for his sins when the Sanhedrin sent him to be executed by Pilot? Was Germany dispensing divine wrath to Israel, Poland, etc., when they plotted to take over the world and exterminate all non-Aryans? Should a German Christian have supported the efforts of the Nazis (who were obviously "God's appointed ambassadors" . . . c'mon, Dad, Romans 13!) knowing that Adolf Hitler was an ambassador of God? If Christ's moral message was only for individuals, and not for groups/nations then why do we think abortion is a social evil (on moral grounds)? A nation is composed of individuals, and while I am not trying to contradict Paul (the State certainly does have the sword for a reason), I am trying to say that the State does not have a license to do anything it wants . . . and when we are ordered by the State to violate God's law, we must not bow to Baal. Civil disobedience is just as mandatory as civil subservience. It all must pass through the filter of conscience, not to mention Christ's mandate that we recognize that the Kingdom has already come. We are now its citizens. There is a real discussion to be had about mercy and justice, and the role (in the right proportion and context) of the State to dispense justice (even imperfect justice). But we are under no obligation to abdicate conscience on behalf of the State.

love,
joshua

Thoughts from a Christian American Soldier:

This morning I awoke wrecked by anxiety. For a full two hours I could not move. From the moment I opened my eyes all I could think of was failure, contradiction, falsity. For the past week or so I have been writing a script to help chronicle my experiences of war, and so for the past few days I have watched films such as Saving Private Ryan, Band of Brothers, and Platoon as a means to help narrate what I experience. After watching films such as these, hearing the first-hand accounts of my forebears' tales of war, it seems to me as if "war" is not even a term I know how to use to describe my time here in the desert. War is supposed to be the threat of being easily annihilated, not the threat of annihilating with ease.

The sacrifices made by my forebears from the Second World War are hard to comprehend. The beaches of Normandy. The winter journey to Berlin. The jungles of Guadalcanal. The massive force of destruction that they had to endure day in and day out in WWII is something I see now but in fragments in the attempts of an impoverished opposition setting off mortar attacks in one or two-round bursts every other day. One of us is killed for about every 40 of them. Or there are the inter-tribal kidnappings, the ransoms that go to fund the resistance. The chaos is real, but I view it mostly from an ivory tower. The utter contradiction and hopelessness levied against my forebears in Vietnam—well-intending American men walking footpaths each day under orders that came to embody the very barbarism they sought to overthrow—I do not palpably sense or encounter here. I have my own paradoxes of barbarism, but the gravity is altogether different. My job is often grueling and mentally and emotionally exasperating, but I live in a place with bins full of the remains of packages sent from home that simply can't be consumed by individual soldiers. This cannot be true of everywhere on the battlefield, but in my corner of the world we have buffets with consumer response cards, air conditioning and internet cafes. I have been injured once, but only because I accidentally stabbed myself with a knife while cutting open a footlocker to pack all of the excess things I could not find a place to store in my living quarters. I am more likely to struggle from putting on weight than from losing it, from spending my money unwisely than from fear of not having a use for it, and from wasting my free time in entertainment than from waiting anxiously for the few times I am afforded it. Even the Eucharist sometimes feels like a product I am given, a thing consumed for the maintenance of morale. This experience of "war" is confusing at best.

Before I became a cadet at West Point, I read a quote of a military statesman who wrote, "I study politics and war, so that my sons may study mathematics and music." This was written hundreds of years ago, but I read it on a brochure for an academy I was then to attend in the coming months. Long before I ever decided to leave the Academy I remember thinking it ironic that I too would be going on to study, yet again, politics and war. Would it be in the hope that one day my children might gain the opportunity to study mathematics and music? For then one must ask, "When will that day come?"

I recently made a man cry. I told him in Arabic that he was not a criminal and not a terrorist. He later told me that he had cried because it was the first time in many months an American soldier, or anyone for that matter, had told him that he was not an evil man. The next day I thundered away at a different man who sat blankly calm with the knowledge that his lies could possibly put the man who had the previous day cried openly in front of me in prison for the greater portion of his life. And now I am faced with the decision of having to abandon their cases altogether, because my job as an interrogator is not the enforcement of justice in criminal investigations, but merely obtaining intelligence relevant to the war-fighting efforts of US Forces.

The other day, one of my superiors talked to my interrogation team prior to a session. He told me, "These are the agents of Satan, gentlemen, they would rather slit your throat and die trying than spend the rest of their lives with the virgin they married the first time around—their wives." It was now my turn to be the blank, expressionless one. This was a Christian man telling me this, obviously trying to impress upon me the reality of a Jihadist's belief in a paradise with 70 virgins and the like. But believing that evil is real does not mean that it is okay to believe that there are those who can completely be its embodiment. When the President stood in the National Cathedral and spoke about the moral dimensions of the war on terrorism, it was not a moment for Christians to show solidarity in the "identification of evil," but a moment for Christians to repent in their having objectified it in the bodies of men. To believe that there are evil men only to be destroyed is to utterly disbelieve in the power of the Resurrection. Anne Lamott wrote, "You can safely assume that you've created God in your own image when it turns out that God hates all the same people you do."

To the legalist-extremist Muslim, evil is something that can be eliminated by eliminating the "evil-doer." If a woman is perceived as indecent, kill her. If a man commits apostasy, kill him. I fear that the West has also adopted this view in certain of its policies to attempt to "rid the world of terror." Evil cannot be destroyed by the destruction of things or persons, it can only be redeemed by those willing to lay down themselves for others. Evil has no existence of itself, it is simply the consequence of an amnesiac and bereft people. Goodness forgotten is goodness perverted. We must be that much more fervent in remembering and reiterating God's initial words over His creation: "It is Good." When we know not what we do, God grant us the grace to forgive, so that we might in turn remember how we, too, once were forgiven.

Every day I talk with the enemy. But, I do not see an embodiment of "he who opposes goodness." If we approach the war on terrorism with the fervor of a Christian Jihad against Islam, our battle is already lost, for we have become what we opposed and we are now the fundamentalists. Our battle is not one of flesh and blood, but against the spiritual powers and principalities which rule this present darkness. We cannot allow ourselves to be caught up in "war mode" against a fleshly enemy, or the true enemy is already within us, and we have failed to believe in the power of a redemption which (we say) we believe has saved us. As James has told us, "faith without works is dead."

Orwell once said that we sleep comfortably in our beds because violent men are willing to conduct violence on our behalf. Uncomfortably I have known this to be true, yet I am also quite guilty of having fallen in step with the pathology of a blood-purchased liberty and self-sanctification. My comfort and liberty must not be won by the sacrifices of a new and foreign poor now paying the price for our moral failings of diplomacy, economy and statesmanship, turning our Republic into an Empire. The memory of those who willingly died in WWII is tarnished every time we resurrect them as an analogy to our alleged "war against terror and tyranny."

A fallen world demands the imposition of justice and the rule of law, but evil cannot be destroyed, it can only be redeemed.

In Him,
joshua

Jacob,

I'm sorry for sounding antagonistic, but I have an M16 strapped to me everywhere I go, and the information I write in reports often leads to people's death and incarceration. I form friendships with Iraqis and then am quite often frightened over whether they are collecting information on my whereabouts in order to aim mortars at me at night. I need people to dialogue with me over this. I'm turning into an ideologue over here because I can read Aristotle and Hauerwas and pissed off "religious left" articles in Sojourners Magazine, but this is serious fucking shit and at just about every turn I feel like my whole fucking faith is being compromised, and at the same time it seems to me that somebody's got to be willing to enter systems of injustice in order to redeem from within. The messiah complex and subsequent guilt then becomes incredibly acute for me, and yet, isn't this our calling? We all have a messianic call-ing. I'm writing because I need help from people I trust.

love,
joshua

FROM ··JOSHUA

SENT ································09/12/2004 08:42PM

TO··JFLO

SUBJECT···················RE: ... PART V CONTINUED

First off, I love you, too. I'm sorry.

I so desperately want someone to follow, Jacob. I just want a sage to come and say, "I've been there before, this is the right path." Why do I feel that that sage just isn't there?

Yesterday morning I awoke to the sounds of mortars, machine gun fire, and automatic grenade launchers. Automatic grenade launchers, Jacob! A rag-tag insurgent attempt to blow up the prison wall was put down in 30 seconds by Marine guards. The news made it seem like the attack was "intense" and "vicious." But Ahmed and Yasser probably planned out yesterday's attacks for 4 months before the Marines blew them all to hell in 30 seconds. And by mid-morning I was emailing, drinking coffee, and buying non-alcoholic beer from our post exchange. 30 seconds.

I received a package yesterday from River of Life, my parents' church. It had everything in it, even a CD player and a Jeremy Camp album. It was great, really. These people really care, and I'll make sure to thank them appropriately. I've only three days now begun again to say the day's liturgy. But liturgy seems self-indulgent to me, like it will delude me from the crap going on— I ask for safety and blessing while Ahmed and Yasser get blown to smithereens. The confusion, the narcissism, the indifference, the desire for good, the utter contradiction is just paralyzing, Jacob. I'm really trying, but it's just a freaking mess.

I (perhaps insanely) volunteered to offer my linguist skills to the light infantry units that do patrols and searches, most of whom have no linguists ever. I did that partly out of boredom, partly out of a feeling of uselessness here (since I have a personal interpreter for every interrogation), partly in order to feel like I have a better understanding of what goes on out beyond the walls, partly because I know that I have a skill which could be very useful in separating the wheat from the chaff before they get arrested, and then partly because. . .yesterday I found out that there are armed check points throughout Fallujah (armed by Mujahideen), and my first thought was "why don't we just take them out with Apaches?!" What is happening to me?

love,
joshua

Yesterday I researched "bad guys" for the entirety of the morning. Personalities, groups, structure, command and control. My interrogation was not until the afternoon, so I took the morning to prepare and learn the atmospherics of the battle and area of operation. The day previous we had been attacked at the prison wall. I woke up to the sound of mortar explosions. We hear explosions all the time, so I continued to go about my business. To be honest, I wasn't entirely sure the explosions had been directed against us until I heard other people talk about what was going on. When I went back to my room, I heard bursts of machine gun fire, and then finally a barrage of fire followed by an explosion that rocked my room. Through the cracks of window on my wall I could see sparks fly, trailed by a cloud of thick black smoke.

A group of vehicles had attempted an attack on the prison. The beginning of the attack had been indirect fire, mortars. This was to be followed up by a suicide bomber driving a truck loaded with explosives—he was going to try to ram the wall and blow a hole in our outer perimeter. Similar plans took form at other locations around the Baghdad area. All in all, this was a fairly complicated attack in the world of insurgent warfare.

But the Marines standing guard on the prison walls ended this attack in minutes, maybe even seconds. The large explosion which rocked my room was the obliteration of the suicide bomber, after the Marines barraged him with 50-cal machine gun fire and Mark-19s (an automatic grenade launcher capable of about 450 rounds per minute—grenades per minute). The vehicle was obliterated. Our wall, intact. The news talked about the fierce fighting which took place in Baghdad. The Marines decimated this uprising during the time it took me to shave a day-old beard.

And as I studied insurgents and their organizations, the morning after this feebly executed attack, my anxiety continued to grow.

As I read alone in my room, I'd look down at my watch—12:10. I'd read some more then look back at my watch—12:35. I had an interrogation at 1:30, yet my anxiety seemed simply to undo me. The purpose of my upcoming interrogation was to reassert control, reassess, find the missing links, extract the needed information. 12:42. I didn't know what was coming over me. It was minutes past when I ought to have already left in order to make it back to the office to resume my planning and prep. But I sat in my chair in a dark room illuminated only by a clip-lamp while I nibbled on dry fruit and chips, continuing to read only because I was terrified to go back to my job.

I then made a decision to forego the interrogation in order to talk with the Chaplain. My interrogation partner agreed to take over for me in my stead, and I went to search out Chaplain Fischer—a young First Lieutenant not that much older than me, but a deeply and sincerely Christian man situated in a much different place in the military, who I thought might offer the kind of counsel that perhaps my proximity to my own circumstances couldn't afford. We talked, prayed, I vexed, and I summoned whatever strength we could conclude upon to go back to my interrogation, take over and finish what I had previously planned. And I did so with relative ease. Instinct is a pretty keen ally. He prayed me back into combat. I was no longer afraid to demand authority, to play upon certain weaknesses of my detainee, and to question in a most heated fashion—because ultimately, I thought, it would lead me to a more accurate assessment of the veracity of his statements. I transgressed no lines of "proper conduct," but I certainly, and without hesitation, used a man's anxieties, weaknesses and fears, and my particular place of power and dominance to assess him according to his word. And then I left, thoroughly relieved to have that moment behind me. And I even left with what I thought was a clearer picture of the man I was assessing—perhaps to his benefit. So, why did I feel like a complete failure?

Jesus did not speak in the imperative when he gave his Sermon on the Mount, he did not say, "Be poor! Be hungry! Get slapped around!" as if to give us instructions on how to counter the world's claims. Jesus indicated that in the world run by God—in the real world—those who are poor ARE those who are valued, those who are hungry and those who thirst for righteousness ARE those who will be satisfied, and those who make peace, who turn the other cheek, ARE those great in the Kingdom of God. Jesus told us that power, influence, position, and violence are not the governing dynamics of reality, but are instead false perversions of the reality made manifest in Christ.

"Blessed are the poor in spirit—for theirs is the kingdom of heaven. Blessed are they that mourn—for they shall be comforted. Blessed are the meek—for they shall inherit the earth. Blessed are they which hunger and thirst after righteousness— for they shall be filled. Blessed are the merciful—for they shall obtain mercy. Blessed are the pure in heart—for they shall see God. Blessed are the peacemakers—for they shall be called the children of God. Blessed are they which are persecuted for righteousness' sake—for theirs is the kingdom of heaven . . . Let your light so shine before men, that they may see your good works, and glorify your Father which is in heaven."

Chaplain Fischer didn't pray me back to the Gospel. He prayed me back into combat.

Bex, you do realize that I don't actually want our Apaches to just "take out" the check points, right? I wrote about that to say how fucked-up my strategizing was. And . . . about Iraq— it's not a monolithic nation. It's filled with many tribes and religions and interests, some sided with the Coalition, some against it. We never understood the diversity here, the many Muslim societies and alliances, regarding the intrusion of the American forces. We are inept at understanding Arabs, or understanding the effect of putting desperate people under extreme pressure. What was needed (above all) was patience, and understanding. Most of the hard-core militants, like the ones at the armed check points, are foreigners come specifically to fight Jihad. Belief is a luxury of those on the sidelines. Money pours in from Saudi Arabia, Syria, Yemen . . . mostly Saudi Arabia. This nation is far from liberated, but I think that the problem has much less to do with the military occupation (as such) than it does with economic warring between

Western and Middle Eastern nations, notably the us and Saudi Arabia, over a turf war being fought just as ruthlessly by Muslims/Middle Easterners as by Christians/Westerners. The problem is so much deeper and more vicious than "unilateralism." This is not simply a "sinfulness of man" problem. Geopolitical strategizing (as such) and the entire political will-to-power is the problem. It's giving in to this myth, the myth that a "greater good" can be won by accepting the powers that be. The blood's on all of us. The sickening part of the politicking is that people think it is a good answer to "soften" military action. If we can just make this or that maneuver "more humane," then we've solved it "enough." We are so sick, and really need to be dropping to our knees.

love,
joshua

Tonight I'm roaming the dustbowl of Abu Ghraib because I can't sleep. As soon as the windstorms of the day end, the helicopters come at night to ensure stillness never arrives. I'm too busy even to remember to puke . . . what a clanging gong I've been this past week or so. We're suspect. I'm suspect. Does the upside-down world preach reform from the inside out? Does it say to make a contribution to your army unit so that people will desire more to abide by the Geneva Conventions, or does it say leave your unit so that your unit feels the lack?

Jacob, I want to be quiet for a long time. I know that's kind of like saying I want to become a cow, because I'm not quiet. I'm never quiet. But I'm so tired. I'm so tired of the opposition, of being opposed to something. I am not free. I am anything but free, I'm shackled by my opposition, or at least so it seems.

Remember the man who came to Christ and called him "Good master." Christ replied, "why do you call me 'Good', for none

85

is Good but God." I've hated that verse for a few years now. It's like, what the f——, Jesus! Of all the things a person would think to have had "right" it would be calling the f-ing SON OF GOD "good." But, nope, wrong again. I know that Christ was probably getting at the motives of the speaker and what the speaker was trying to "get from" Christ, through flattery or something . . . but it seems to symbolize what seems like a bottomless rabbit hole of "good." What in fact is "good"? Right now, these are questions which leave me paralyzed in a dark room, only to run on auto pilot as I enter an interrogation 20 minutes late, harass an innocent man, and feel a fraud as soon as I leave.

And then I stay up at night because I don't want the next day to come. I am NOT free. I just don't know if I in fact AM my own problem . . . or rather, to what extent I am my own problem.

I finished The Cost of Discipleship and I've started reading Bonhoeffer's Ethics . . . and it's f-ing unbelievable, Jacob. Bonhoeffer melds together the classical with the revelational, the intellectual with the scriptural, the particular with the universal, Wittgenstein and Derrida with Aquinas and Kant! Well, I draw the postmodern connections myself . . . but, he's so far ahead of himself it's beautiful. And I feel on the edge of myself when reading him. I almost started crying today. I brought the book into the interrogation booth, hiding for the 45 minutes prior to my session as I delved into incarnational ethics and the ineffability of that nebulous thing called "the will of God." And then I talked to a man about how our joint venture in killing someone wanted by him and by his tribe and by the Coalition (well, we "think" it's the same guy . . . but, if it's not, who cares . . .) would be a good thing . . . how we could, say, hi-five each other over the thought of each party assisting the other in vengeance and military expediency (I think we call this "justice"). Wow! What a partnership! I convinced a man to help us help him in committing vengeful murder. Anyone wanna go to a praise and worship service with me tonight? Maybe we can take the Eucharist together? Let's sit down at a "Purpose Driven Life" 40 Days of Purpose Bible study and talk about "divine mercy" and "God's will for my life." God have mercy on my soul.

love,
joshua

Jesus didn't advocate "passivism," but "pacifism" ... he made manifest in his incarnation "redemptive suffering." That's an incredibly active endeavor, anything but passive.

There is also a difference between "force" and "lethal force." Playing football or learning boxing isn't what this is all about. But, when our aggressiveness is not used in love (especially) with our enemies, then we ought not even think of our families as property to claim, our "entitlement to defend." In Christianity there are no "rights" because there is nothing ever to lose, nothing to demand ... we've been given everything already. Anyone who dies for Christ's sake will live, even (especially) the innocent. Those who lose their lives for My sake, will gain them. Not everyone who says unto me Lord, Lord shall enter into the Kingdom of Heaven, but he that doeth the will of my Father which is in heaven.

All our actions are active, but they must rely (practically, not just poetically) upon God's divine action. We are participants, but never lords. Not sure if that clears anything up . . . what do you think?

love,
joshua

"You are his voice of love"?

Dad, I don't know what you conceive war-fighting consisting of, but it's fucking dirty! I am constantly falsely accusing people of things, using a man's emotions of vengeance for self-gain. I am an intimate partner in the killing of men without trial.

You are entirely correct to state that New Testamental ethics is given to the Christian, and not to the State. But you're going to have to search really hard in the New Testament to find even an inkling of evidence that Christians are supposed to consider themselves the recipients of the authority of Romans 13 . . . as if we are the ones charged with the rule of nations and with the assumption of the responsibilities of carrying the sword. It just isn't there, from Matthew to Revelation, it is not there. For the first 300 years of Christianity if you wanted to be baptized you had to forfeit certain positions in society. Other than the obvious "moral" ones (prostitution, pimping, etc.), almost any position that ruled by means of power had to be forfeited before baptism was even granted. Back then it meant that military, police, judges, and others WERE the recipients of Romans 13 authority. The State has a legitimate use of the sword, but Christians are told over and over again to be subservient, to be submissive (not just in "heart," but practically also) by forfeiting their claims to power. And so, we don't take people to court, we don't take up the sword, we don't resist the evil doers . . . you know, that whole "Jesus thing."

And rescinding my oath of enlistment is not even in the same ballpark as a person rescinding marriage vows in divorce. Joining the army is not a sacrament, it's a pagan allegiance.

joshua

FROM ··· JOSHUA
SENT ······························· 10/10/2004 3:48 AM
TO ··· HOME
SUBJECT ······················· RE: FW: GREAT ARTICLE

Dad,

My statement about "easy" choices is not to say that war is somehow not difficult. It's more along the lines of what CS Lewis described in his discourses on pain. Lewis said that "pain is God's megaphone to a deaf world," it's His call to us to grow up, to venture out into the world of others. It's our call to maturity, to empathy, to love. When faced with danger and with violence, the instinctual and immediate response is "stop the violence!" That's not bad, in itself. The desire to protect the innocent is not bad in itself. The way that we fix the problem, our method for solving this new-found pain, is what we must question. We must at least allow the pain inflicted upon us by our enemies to be a megaphone to our own deafness to the world, waking us up to the needs of others, to the violence inflicted upon them. Do we choose maturity, or simply to stop the pain?

Soldiers. Soldiers are indeed a grand example of sacrifice. It's simply a tragedy that this is so . . . because we have built up so many thick hedges around ourselves that we covet "security" to the point of paranoia. The most valued people in society are those who maintain this security through violence. We have virtually no other selfless people because we're too concerned with being selfish and protecting what is ours . . . our land, our "liberty," our "way of life"—and we do all this under a perversion of Romans 13, which is a reminder to the Christians that the State serves a purpose (perhaps being the contrast to the love of Christ's Kingdom), and not to usurp that power, because Christ will use it for His purposes. But Romans 13 is certainly not a call for Christians to rule. Even after Constantine's "conversion" he did not get baptized, because he thought that a person in his position could not at the same time be an emperor and also a "Christian."

Now, perhaps I will have to finish my tour as a non-combatant, perhaps outright discharge. I can't see the Chaplaincy happening because my general convictions about the distinction between Church and State are too radical for any sort of coherent pastoral role. But I am absolutely convinced that service in my current way is absolutely wrong, and totally outside the bounds of the witness of the New Testament. If people do not understand this uncompromising allegiance, and think me a deserter, so be it. Having made mistakes in the past is not an excuse to continue to make them now over fear of "misunderstanding."

I'm not at the end of the road yet on what exactly my conviction, my understanding of a call to discipleship means. But I will take deadly serious Christ's call to Peter that he drop his nets and follow. I cannot continue as an American war fighter. I just won't, Dad. It sickens me day in and day out, and it's treason against my King, against my real Kingdom and home. I will think long and hard about whether completing my term of service as a non-combatant is necessary.

We are a light unto the nations, so give unto Caesar what is Caesar's and unto God what is God's. But I have given unto Caesar what is in fact God's, and I don't care what anyone thinks about taking action to set my allegiances straight. I made a decision in youth, almost 8 years ago. I wanted to do as you had done, as your dad had done. I wanted to wear the clothes of a leader. I am no longer a child, and will not continue to act as if I am. I've been wearing this clothing of leadership for eight years, but my desire was to become a leader—even if that now means shedding the uniform. I am not running from what is hard, Dad, but rather strapping myself to a new cross, for walking in faithfulness to this purpose will be much harder than what any army can conceive. People will probably try to test my pacifism, perhaps even do violence against me. And I will have to let them without striking back. People will look to my lifestyle, to see if I'm reaping the benefits of a comfortable American existence ... i.e., the proceeds of our violence. And I must be a force of redemption from within, not indulging in such comforts, but using them for the good of others.

love,
joshua

FROM ·· REBA

SENT ····························· 10/11/2004 1:30 PM

TO ··· JOSHUA

SUBJECT ································· DERRIDA

I assume you've heard?

> Europe: French Philosopher
> Jacques Derrida Dies in Paris
> VOA News
> 09 Oct 2004,
> Jacques Derrida

French philosopher Jacques Derrida has died at the age of 74. Friends of the philosopher say he died of cancer late Friday in a Paris hospital.

Born in Algeria in 1930, Mr. Derrida studied at the Sorbonne before starting a teaching career there and at American universities.

Mr. Derrida is best known as the founder of the deconstructionist school of philosophy, which sees the meaning of a text as not definite and unchanging but dependent on how a reader interprets it.

Last night I went through a base defense plan, toting my M16 down hallways with a flashlight yelling "CLEAR!" At every corner was a lieutenant in the background talking about firing twice to the chest, once to the forehead. This morning gunfire erupted like a hurricane just outside my wall. AK-47s, 50-cals, SAWs, the works. Tracers flew above the perimeter, inside the prison. Cigarette smoke drifted from my mouth last night as the first day of Ramadan came to a close. Three meals sat in my belly, and a friend brought cookies and water to my defensive position as we trained for the real thing that came this morning.

I am always asking myself questions of meaning, and they really have nothing to do with war or Iraq. Does this activity have any meaning? Phrases from books will walk alongside me as I go. Moses and Tolkien sit next to me, and when I cannot put words to deeds, some story to narrate my motions, I fight the temptation to shut off my mind so as not to hear the silence. Between action and thought I am usually left at the place of memory, wondering about the wheres and whys of my past, and how this now of mine relates to the wheres and whys of my future. What seems infinite I have to digest through the finite bits I can comprehend, and the ever-changing now-turned-future is revealed unto me, always, so it seems, by means of the past. I know who I am and where I am going by the act of remembering.

Last week I awoke with a memory. I remembered a certain desire I had to travel to Paris, to study under a man whom I had come to admire greatly, a philosopher named Jacques Derrida. I am not at all certain why, but for some reason it occurred to me that, in his aging, he might soon die. It troubled me for a moment, thinking of a potentially unfulfilled wish, but then the grief, along with the moment, passed. About an hour later, I learned from my sister in an email that Derrida had in fact died.

I always felt connected to Derrida's writings. His words took a certain life inside of me, which I felt connected the two of us. I would read him like one who believes. But it's perhaps more truthful to say that Derrida is much more important to me not in what he said, but in what he did. The gift Derrida gave me was the conundrum of silence. Derrida coined a phrase: "The End of Books and the Beginning of Writing." In a way I have seen this as similar to another phrase coined by St. Francis of Assisi: "Preach the Gospel always and when necessary use words." Derrida talked of bringing to an end the idea of always looking to previously spoken ideas eternally enscripted within "books" as ends in themselves, self-contained parcels of truth. St. Francis, in his own Christian way, said the same—the idea is less important than how it is made manifest in the transformation of your life. Or, perhaps—put down the book and write good news through the life you live!

In reading Derrida, I could not help but notice my own distance from myself when looking into a mirror. I could not help but notice my continual pondering over a knowledge of good and evil phrased in the third person. What is good for one to do? What and how ought one to love? I could sense a separation from myself in my kneeling before the many systems of thought I used to describe myself and others. A certain self-violence seemed a part of my vision, my speech, and the way I heard and felt the world around me.

The madness of a rehearsed violence struck with force as I sat and breathed beneath a gaze of stars that covered still the wordless movements of those about me. A kind of ignorance seemed to permeate our rehearsals for battle—not ignorance of action, but ignorance of something else. Smoke rose from the earth and my lips, the Muezzins called men to piety. Chemicals and blind action allowed my eyes to remain vigilant. And I walked in the duties of survival, practicing with my body to separate friend from foe, me from them. There must be somewhere a memory, I thought, to locate me beyond this, beyond me even.

So, I just experienced why it is I am here in Iraq. Other than all the struggles I've been wrestling with . . . I just "met" my reason—a young foreign jihadist who said he might kill me if he had the chance (that is, as long as I am a US soldier in Muslim lands). The Gospel came out of his mouth unwittingly, while trying to convert me to Islam. It was beautiful. I was dumbstruck. I left praising Christ, and thanking God for this enemy. I confessed to him my sins, and asked him to look at his own. I'm certain that this interrogation was not "doctrinal" by Army standards. Pardon my bluntness, but to hell with the Army and their "doctrines." Today was a moment when life mattered! I did not try to justify myself but instead asked God (and my enemy) simply for mercy. What is terrifying is that this jihadist genuinely wanted my conversion—for me to see the emptiness of "American beauty"—he talked of the peace and happiness I would find in "true religion." And I felt him actually care for me, desire for my good. I asked him why he came to Iraq to kill, and then he asked me why I did. "Your Lord, our prophet Isa, tells you to turn the other cheek, to love those who hate you. Why do you not do this?" I replied, "You're right," and then asked him when he would "go and do likewise." He said vengeance was his right. I lacked the power to challenge him in any way that I did not challenge myself, because such ideas of "love" and "forgiveness" and "compassion" are not fully manifest and incarnate in me, tangibly and practically to be seen and felt—as if to say, "LOOK at the love I give you." After all was said and done, we ended with a feeling of mutual respect. I left and I prayed I would be given the chance to see him one day in the future when I could say, "I left that world behind me, so can you."

love,
joshua

Joshua, Please refrain from sending me any more examples of the Narcissistic Personality. The degree of your present self-absorption is indicative of a spiritual sickness that issues forth into the betrayal of many. And besides, I am presently trying to help soldiers and sailors whose obedience and humility reveal much more of Jesus to me than your psychic journey through cloud-cookooland. FM

FROM ···JOSHUA

SENT·······························10/29/2004 12:42 PM

TO ···HOME

SUBJECT···

Today the rains fell. Explosions jolted the ground sporadically all throughout the day. Yesterday an explosion erupted so severely I could feel the air within my ears pulsate. The sound seemed muffled, as if from a distance, while the sheer bass of the explosion moved through me with an eerie expediency. Later I learned that eight Marines had died merely kilometers from the prison walls. And all throughout the day rain fell while explosions rocked the earth beneath me.

We become accustomed to mortar fire. We become accustomed to the medevac helicopters overhead. We become accustomed to the intelligence brief summaries. Body counts, target acquisitions. In between interrogations and report writing I sat outside today beneath a tactical canopy, drinking cold coffee and smoking a small brown Dominican-leaf cigarillo. And the rains simply continued to fall.

Last night I watched The Thin Red Line with two friends. A young Private tells Sean Penn about how he was beaten as a child, but that in this war he is living by the second. He thought it couldn't get any worse than his father, but here "there's only God and dying—that's all there is." My friend asked me if I thought I would be like that Private if I went out to fight—religious and shuddering. I told him I didn't know, but that I would like to think I'd rather be like the Captain whose Battalion Commander thought him a coward for refusing a direct order he believed would have killed the men and boys of his command. I like to think that would be me . . . but I don't know, I told him. I don't know.

A woman today told me, "you like the word pious, don't you? I've heard you describe these guys like that a lot . . . you like that word, good word." I told her that it's a word I have discovered I most often use to describe Muslims and Catholics. I don't describe Evangelical Christians as "pious" and I don't refer to Buddhists or Sikhs that way, either. Perhaps it is how medievalism came to shape both the major religions, Islam and Catholicism. Medieval "piety" as perhaps opposed to "devotion" or "sincerity."

I recently spoke with an Iraqi Muslim man who sells DVD's at the prison. We talk every time we see each other—he always tries to encourage me in my Arabic speaking. He showed me pictures of his wife, son and two daughters. I told him his youngest daughter looks like him, while his son has the look of his mother. He nodded his head in approval. I felt the small maroon folding wallet in my pocket with the pictures most meaningful to me. I told him to go in peace, and then returned to my desk to prepare for the following day.

FROM ··JOSHUA
SENT··································11/01/2004 7:42 PM
TO··JFLO
SUBJECT·························... BUELLER? BUELLER?

To a slightly smaller "all":

The skies just parted and Elijah, Moses and Jesus Christ the Lord descended from the heavens! I'll be home from January 14–30 ... and my commander and I just had "the talk." I was on night guard duty, and my commander was up late doing some work ... so, he sticks his head around the corner and asks if I want to knock out change-of-command "initial counseling." (Just to orient you to the amazing timing of this, it was just today (today!!!) that I decided to tell my battalion chaplain of my intentions to apply for Conscientious Objector status.) So, when my commander asked me into his office during my guard shift, I just looked up, took a deep breath, made the sign of the cross and said, "and so it begins ... God help me."

He totally supports me and said he wants to do everything he can to help me in my transition out of the Army ... it was amazing! I mean, it seemed almost unreal. He told me he thought I was one of the best interrogators under his command, that he very much appreciated the way I have handled my duties in light of my ethical dilemmas, that he has been nothing but impressed with my nobility, leadership and maturity (good thing he doesn't read my tempestuous emails!), and that I am the interrogator with the greatest knowledge of Arabs, the greatest sensitivity and creativity, outright. Needless to say, I was pretty dumbstruck. When I left West Point, my commander basically told me I was worthless. I've been pretty scared to start this ball rolling because of that, as if this is leaving West Point all over again. This time, however, my present commander called me courageous and said he admired my willingness to follow after my convictions regardless of opposition.

So . . . it's done. Getting the support of the command is THE ENTIRE BATTLE. It's basically done. He said he'd find out for me how I can get a head start on the paperwork even while still in Iraq, so that when I make it back to the States I can hit the ground running. I'm telling you, this conversation was raw and intimate and compelling and. . .it was amazing!

love,
joshua

Cherie,

Belief that there is a plan that is greater than this war is the only thing that keeps me sane. I have lost and gained weight over and over again here trying to think anew each day how I can possibly continue to be a light, to do my job with Christian integrity. I don't complain about "the military" because of inconvenience or discomfort, Cherie. I complain about how perilous it feels to attempt an authentic Christianity in the midst of "exploiting persons of their intelligence value," and then listening to the news, hearing of the bombing campaign just undertaken in the town that I just wrote an intelligence report on only days previous. Those bombs are given coordinates by my reports. Mine, Cherie.

My issue is not "the war in Iraq," it's Christian complicity in sin. It's MY complicity in systems of sin and violence. Isn't it possible to say, "there is a perfect path, come join us. Do as we do. It was made manifest in and shown to us by Christ, and continued by the Apostles and the Church. WE are that Church today, come join our community." THAT is what I wanted to say to the Jihadist. To everyone here. To the entire world. There is another way. Violence and coercion are not the true nature of the reality where faith, hope and love reign. Do we actually believe that?

in Him,
joshua

POST-DEPLOYMENT TO IRAQ

202nd Military Intelligence Battalion

FORT GORDON, GA

Hey, David.

Sorry I've been offline for so long. Kuwait was a nice quiet respite before coming home, but actually returning isn't proving easy. Coming home to the welcome parade felt like stepping into the twilight zone. I had to remind myself to smile so that my family and friends wouldn't feel too worried about me. But I spent most of the evening avoiding eye contact and staring at the exit signs. I'm no longer in a combat zone, but in some ways everything seems harder and less clear. When you've got violence all around, clarity is easy—do what you must. But the day after we arrived back I found myself at a mini mall trying on a leather jacket that my sister wanted to buy me as a late Christmas present. Two days earlier I'd been in Kuwait, toting an M16; three weeks before that, in Iraq strapped in body armor and aiming that same M16 at little boys. I don't know how to go from flack vests and assault rifles to fashion cycle jackets in what seems like overnight. Part of me almost wants to go back—to have the clarity of opposition. I talk on email or on the phone infrequently. I take lots of drives. I buy things I don't need. My friends and I drink more than we used to. It was one thing to come to a place of moral clarity about what I am not, but that does not settle for me what I am— much less, who I am. The ideological questions seem less important. Or, perhaps they seem so obvious that it seems like madness to have been distracted from the simple daily issues of life, God, others and love. But that is the world which seems most terrifying to me now.

FROM ···JOSHUA
SENT ···························03/26/2005 5:27 PM
TO ··HOME
CC ······························REBA; NOMI; TRAV
SUBJECT ·········RE: THE ARRIVAL OF CAPTIVATING

Hey, all. My hearing was the other day. To wrap things up regarding how things have gone, I thought I'd include a bit from my CO app. The end is in sight, I feel it. Can't wait to see you with this world behind me.

From my Conscientious Objector application:

... Since the day I walked onto Academy grounds at West Point, I have been in an ongoing and quite conscious battle with my military service. Whether it was my first decision in college to turn away from military service altogether, or my post-September 11th decision to return to service, I have been attempting to mitigate conscience and duty for the past seven years. In the absence of a clear and articulate objection to service, I have defaulted to evolving forms of duty as my guiding principle.

115

My misgivings run much deeper than merely personal distaste for a vocation. It is not "the job" but the institution. My path to conscientious objection has been slow but consistent. Conscientious objection is now the only way dutifully to fulfill my obligations both to faith and to nation, and to my own internal commitments to personal courage.

The only real ethical dilemma I encountered at Fort Huachuca during my training was signing the "consent-to-lie" form. It seemed a backward thing for a Christian to do, on a certain level . . . And, still, the blanket issue of "deception" is not necessarily a theological problem for me, as say "manipulation" is (or as we say in the field, "exploitation"). This is the moral issue, manipulation and exploitation, from which my CO convictions began to crystallize.

My first moral difficulty dealt with deception, and from this issue everything else evolved. From my very first interrogation until now, I have simply lacked the ability to look at the person I interrogate in a way that does not demand I also think about what is best for him. If I cannot run an interrogation approach that will either genuinely help a person's position in life or enlighten that person about some moral issue, I cannot run the approach. I tried many times in my first weeks at Abu Ghraib to be more "strategic," and I attended confession after each of these sessions because of an overwhelming burden to atone for what I considered the sin of reducing individuals to strategic "objects of exploitation." It did not matter if the detainee was a war-hardened jihadist bent upon my destruction or just a wrongly accused farmer, what I discovered in interrogation is that I personally cannot offer an incentive I know I cannot (or will not) actually follow through on, present scenarios that I myself do not believe in, or manipulate preexisting feelings of enmity or create new feelings of enmity in a person for the purposes of "intelligence exploitation." Every time I walk into the interrogation booth I see a man in need of redemption, and because of that I have had to utterly recreate my interrogation methods in order to reconcile the demands of my job with who I am as a person and as a Christian. I am still recreating my methods, and confessing my sins (for as long as the task is mine), having in no way found the answer of how to reconcile these conflicting worlds.

My dilemma is not so much one of moral action, but of sheer IDENTITY ... In Christ God has shown us what it looks like to operate according to the way the world is. The tension of that reality against the powers and principalities which rule is the tension that ultimately led Christ to the cross. And what are we told? "Pick up your cross and follow

117

me today! Do not be conformed to the world, but be transformed in the renewing of your mind! Fear not he who can destroy your body, but he who can destroy your soul! Whoever does not abandon all for my sake is not fit to be my disciple. These things I have spoken unto you, that in me you might have peace. In the world you shall have tribulation: but be of good cheer; I have overcome the world!"

Joshua Casteel

has authored several plays performed in the US and
abroad, including *Returns* and *The Interrogation Room*.
He has given talks on religious and political matters
throughout the United States, Ireland, Sweden,
Italy and the United Kingdom. He currently lives in
Iowa City where he is at work on a memoir.

Essay Press

is dedicated to publishing innovative, explorative,
and culturally relevant essays in book form.
We welcome your support through the purchase
of our books and through donations directly to the
press. Please contact us at essaypress@gmail.com
to be added to our mailing list and visit
www.essaypress.org to learn more about us.

Eula Biss, Stephen Cope, Catherine Taylor EDITORS

New and forthcoming titles from Essay Press:

JENNY BOULLY *The Body: An Essay*

ALBERT GOLDBARTH *Griffin*

CARLA HARRYMAN *Adorno's Noise*

KRISTIN PREVALLET *I, Afterlife:*
Essay in Mourning Time